The World's Fair of 1893:
Ultra Massive Photographic Adventure
Volume 1
Copyright © 2017 Inecom, LLC.
All Rights Reserved

Written and designed by Mark Bussler

www.ClassicGameRoom.com

Other books by Mark Bussler

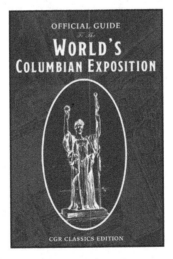

The World's Fair of 1893
Ultra Massive Photographic
Adventure Vol. 3

Official Guide to the
World's Columbian Exposition

The White City of Color: 1893
World's Fair

The Court of Honor

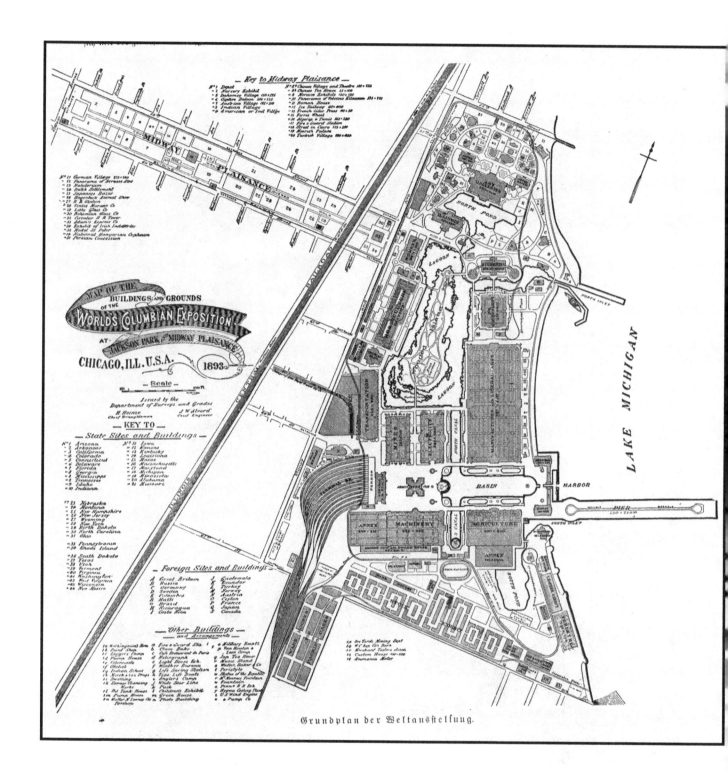

YE SHALL KNOW THE TRUTH AND THE TRUTH SHALL MAKE YOU FREE

TO THE PIONEERS OF CIVIL AND RELICIOUS LIBERTY
BUT BOLDER THEY WHO FIRST OFF-CAST
THEIR MOORINGS FROM THE HABITABLE PAST
AND VENTURED CHARTLESS ON THE SEA
OF STORM-ENGENDERING LIBERTY.

Introduction

In the summer of 1893, the greatest party in the world was thrown in Chicago, Illinois to celebrate the 400th anniversary of Columbus discovering the Americas.

Between May and October of that year, more than 27 million visitors from across the United States and around the world made their way to a reclaimed swampy park on the edge of Lake Michigan. They honored the technical, scientific and cultural achievements of the Western world while indulging in copious amounts of beer and sideshow antics. The World's Columbian Exposition, as it was known, was quite the event.

It's hard to imagine a time when the entire country, let alone the entire world, could get together to celebrate anything in a relatively peaceful manner. It happened, and we have the photographic evidence to prove it. Good times were had in Chicago that summer. So sorry I missed it, my grandparents weren't even born yet.

Plenty has been written about the World's Fair, both fiction and nonfiction. The setting was incredible and, despite the photography, seems unreal. How could this have existed, and why is it no longer there? The fairgrounds were built in a year, on top of pylons driven into the mud by workers without power tools or modern machinery. Just imagine the days before labor laws!

The Fair took place during an era of rapid technological advancement. In the late 19th century, humanity moved into the modern electrical age of lighting, mechanization and mass production. This was one of the first times that light bulbs were used on a large scale. The fair was the debut of much that we take for granted today like the Ferris Wheel.

The fairgrounds were intended to be temporary; nothing remains except for the Palace of Fine Arts which is the modern-day Chicago Museum of Science and Industry. I highly recommend visiting it after enjoying this book because the layout of the grounds remains similar despite the lack of buildings and sculptures.

In a previous life, I was a documentary producer and collected hundreds of books about subjects ranging from World Wars to World's Fairs. My favorite part of researching the 1893 Fair was thinking about what it must have been like to be there.

This book is intended to serve as an entertaining bit of inspiration for your next trip into the land of imagination. It is a record of events that took place long ago.

Perhaps you've read a novel about the fair or seen a film and want to place yourself there. Using the maps and landmarks such as the Grand Basin and Manufacturers and Liberal Arts Building, it is easy to get one's bearings.

It is incomprehensible to fully appreciate what it must have been like to see light-up fountains, spotlights and people from cultures other than your own. There was no Internet; there were no smartphones. This party predates television, radio and even the Atari 2600!

All of these pictures have been meticulously scanned from period books and a collection of historical artifacts. They are laid out in what I perceive as a common-sense way to view the fair. My recommendation is to start at the Court of Honor and slowly meander to the Palace of Fine Arts and Midway, taking in sights along the way.

Personally, I would make a beeline to Old Vienna. I'm confident that one of the photographers spent all of his time there and it looked quite fun. 10 cent sausages is a bargain!

These days I work on the Internet. I'm a writer, photographer, and artist who loves history. I hope that you enjoy this book and see things that you may have never seen before.

Mark Bussler is producer of *Classic Game Room* and writer of the *Ultra Massive Video Game Console Guide* series, *Magnum Skywolf, Ethel the Cyborg Ninja, Lord Karnage, The White City of Color: 1893 World's Fair* and more.

The Peristyle and Liberty

The Court of Honor and Administration Building at night.

The Administration Building

Administration Building at dusk.

Administration Building under construction.

View from atop the Manufacturers Building.

Wooded Island and Lagoon.

View toward Administration Building

Farmer's Bridge.

White Star Building on the right.

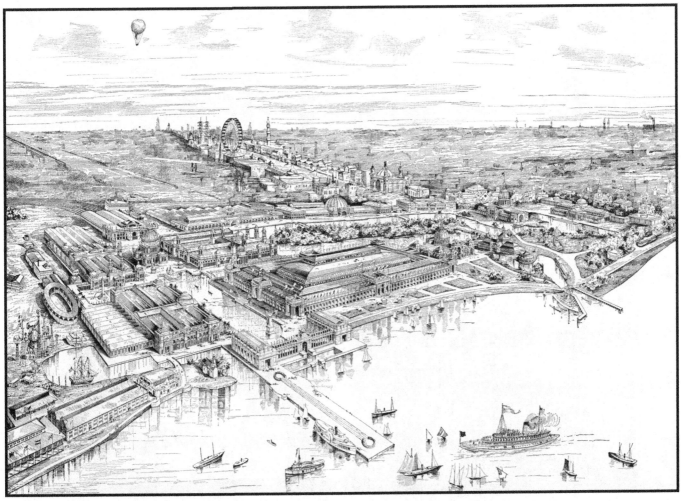

View toward the Colonnade.

The Colonnade.

The arch in the center of the Peristyle.

The Peristyle at night.

Man walks between huge columns of the Peristyle.

The Peristyle arch lit up at night.

Court of Honor as viewed from the Peristyle.

Administration Building at night.

Manufacturers Building at night.

Administration Building at night with fountains.

Boat in front of Manufacturers Building.

Columbian Fountain at night.

View toward Agriculture Building.

Court of Honor looking toward Golonnade.

Court of Honor looking toward Golonnade from farther back.

Agriculture Building at night.

Searchlight on top of Manufacturers Building.

MacMonnies Fountain.

The Quadriga on the Peristyle.

Terminal Station.

Administration.

Columbian Fountain.

Grand Basin and Administration Building.

Colonnade.

View from Southwest corner of Manufacturers.

FOUR HUNDRED YEARS
AFTER THE DISCOVERY
OF THIS CONTINENT BY
CHRISTOPHER COLUMBUS
THE NATIONS OF THE WORLD
UNITE ON THIS SPOT TO
COMPARE IN FRIENDLY EMU
LATION THEIR ACHIEVEMENTS
IN ART SCIENCE MANUFAC
TURES AND AGRICULTURE

Electric fountain at night.

Interior of fountain, working pump valves.

Men working the electric fountain switchboard and reflectors.

Interior of electric fountain, changing the colors.

Interior of electric fountain, color slides and projector.

Interior of electric fountain, signal slides.

Electricity Building at night.

Court of Honor.

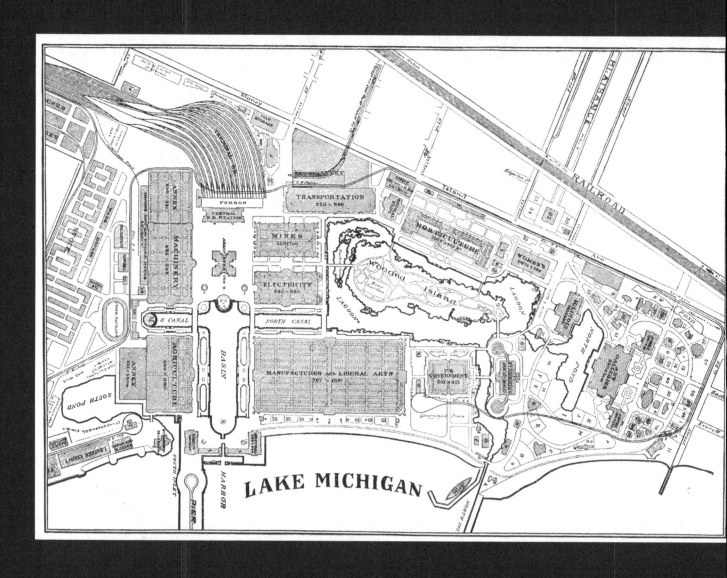

Music Hall, Peristyle and movable sidewalk.

Looking North toward Illinois Building

Boat on lagoon in front of Fisheries.

Terminal Station

Court of Honor.

Panorama of Transportation Building reflecting off the lagoon.

The golden door of the Transportation Building.

Reflection of Transportation Building.

Entrance to Horticulture Building

Northern pavilion of Horticulture Building and exhibit
of hot-houses and summer-houses.

Horticulture Building.

Fish and Fisheries Building.

Entrance to Fish and Fisheries Building.

Fish and Fisheries Building under construction.

Fish and Fisheries Building under construction.

Entrance to Machinery Building

A gondola looking toward Colonnade.

View of the Grand Basin looking North.

Looking North from the Colonnade.

Looking East from Womans Building.

Looking North from Terminal Station.

Looking South from Woman's Building

Looking South from Illinois Building

Looking West from Gafe De Marine.

Feeding the ducks.

Looking West from Peristyle.

The Peristyle and Statue of the Republic.

Administration building. World's Fair

362. From roof of Liberal Arts North. World's Fair.

357 Fine Arts Building, World's Fair

Machinery Hall.

Machinery Hall under construction.

The fairgrounds under construction.

Machinery Hall.

Agriculture Building.

Entrance Agriculture Building

Grand Basin with Agriculture
Building in distance.

View looking North from Administration Building.

Court of Honor and Agriculture Building.

View from balcony of Woman's Building.

The Woman's Building.

The Woman's Building.

The Woman's Building.

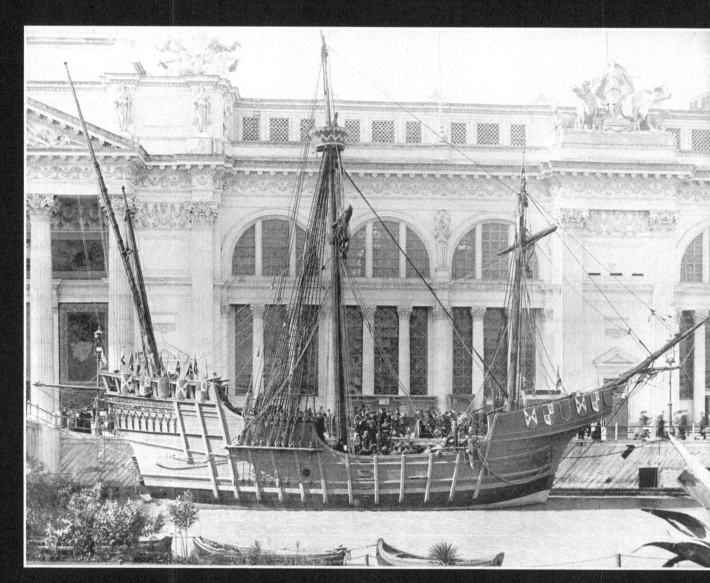

Santa Maria.

Santa Maria.

Santa Maria, interior.

Columbian Exposition:

CHICAGO 1893

145. Government and Fisheries Buildings, World's Fair.

Columbian Exposition:

CHICAGO 1893

Horticulture building from Wooded Island. World's Fair.

395. View from Transportation dome. World's Fair.

Scene from roof of Liberal Arts, World's Fair.

The Mines and Mining Building

Mines and Mining Building.

Mines and Mining under construction.

Mines and Mining Building.

Eastern facade of Mines and Mining Building.

View of Electricity, Mining and Administration.

Electricity Building.

Western facade of Electricity Building.

Eastern facade of Electricity Building.

Electricity Building.

Lagoon behind Electricity Building.

MANZ & Co. CHIC.

Crowd in front of Electricity Building.

Electricity Building entrance.

388, South front of Electricity building, World's Fair.

8437. The Three Fountains, Columbian Exposition.

Wooded Island and Manufacturers and Liberal Arts Building.

Entrance to Manufacturers and Liberal Arts Building.

Manufacturers and Liberal Arts Building.

Northern facade of Manufacturers and Liberal Arts.

Southwest corner Manufacturers and Liberal Arts.

Terminal Station.

Painting above entrance of Manufacturers and Liberal Arts Building

Palace of Fine Arts.

Illinois Building and Palace of Fine Arts.

Palace of Fine Arts.

The White Star Building.

The Puck Building

Electric Railway.

Bureau of Public Gomfort.

Cafe De Marine.

Chocolate Pavilion.

Pennsylvania Railroad Pavilion

PENNSYLVANIA RAILROAD EXHIBIT
STANDARD PNEUMATIC INTERLOCKING SWITCHES AND
SIGNALS WESTINGHOUSE SYSTEM

Krupp Building

On the shore of Lake Michigan.

Pier and movable sidewalk.

The Steamship Michigan.

Pier with movable sidewalk.

Movable sidewalk on the pier.

View from the Ferris Wheel.

Line to board a Ferris Wheel car.

View inside the Ferris Wheel.

8623. In its Glory, World's Columbian Exposition.

7891. View from Island Bridge, World's Fair.

8248. Transportation Building, Columbian Exposition.

8779. Great Fire Works, World's Columbian Exposition.

8333. The King of Old Vienna, Midway Plaisance, Columbian Exposition.

View from the Ferris Wheel.

German Village

German Village

German Beergarden.

German Village.

German village

Old Vienna.

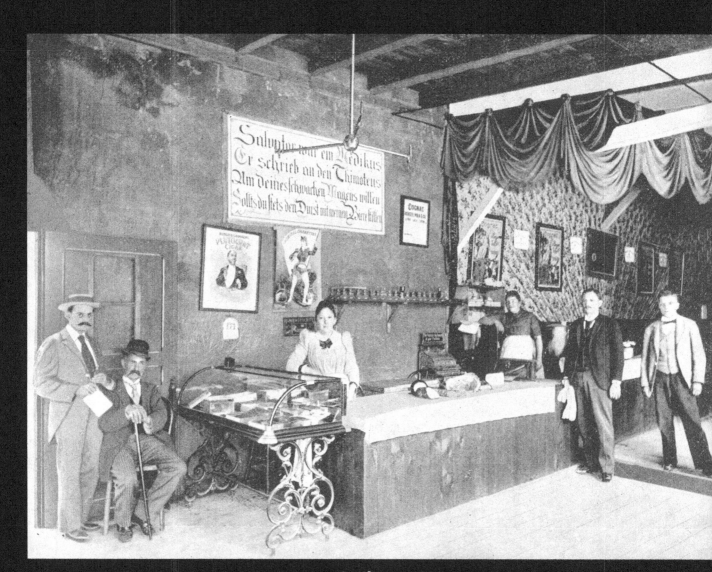

Old Vienna.

A corner shop in old Vienna.

Vienna Confectionery.

Old Vienna

Old Vienna.

Old Vienna.

Old Vienna.

Old Vienna

Old Vienna.

Old Vienna.

Hagenbeck's Arena.

Egyptian Theater.

Egyptian Theater.

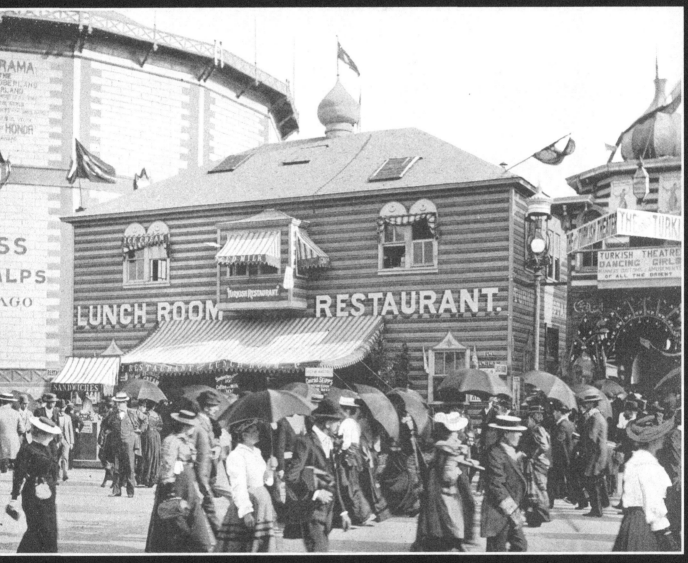

Entrance to the Turkish Theater

Crowds walk in front of the Chinese Theater.

Crowds pass in front of the Irish Village.

The Lapland Village.

Dahomey Village.

Miniature Cathedral of St. Peter.

The Electric Scenic Theater.

Scene in the theater.

Turkish Village.

Java Village

Java Village

Algerian Theater

Persian Theater.

Ladies on the Midway.

East Indian Palace.

South Sea Island Theater.

A crowd on the Midway.

Franco-American Cafe.

Hawaii Palace of Pele.

Irish Village.

Deep sea diving exhibit.

Chinese Theater.

Bulgarian Curiosities.

Swiss Alps panorama on Midway.

Turkish Village.

Interior view Java Theater.

Turkish Bazaar.

COSTUME EXHIBIT

40 NATIONS

OF BEAUTIES.

World's Congress of Beauty.

World's Congress of Beauty.

Libbey Glass Company

Cairo Street on Midway.

CO. CHI.

The Aztec's Village.

Street of Constantinople.

The Brazilian Building.

Victoria House

Canadian Building

The German Building.

Japanese Tea Garden.

Japanese Ho-O-Den.

Japanese Tea Garden.

Venezuela Building.

Guatemala Building.

Costa Rica Building.

Haiti Building.

Ceylon Building.

French Government Building.

Illinois Building.

Indiana Building

Kentucky Building

Massachusetts Building.

New Hampshire Building.

New Jersey Building.

New York Building.

North Dakota Building.

Territorial Building.

Pennsylvania Building.

Iowa Building.

Arkansas Building.

Utah Building.

West Virginia Building.

Connecticut Building.

Kansas Building.

Louisiana Building.

Maine Building.

302

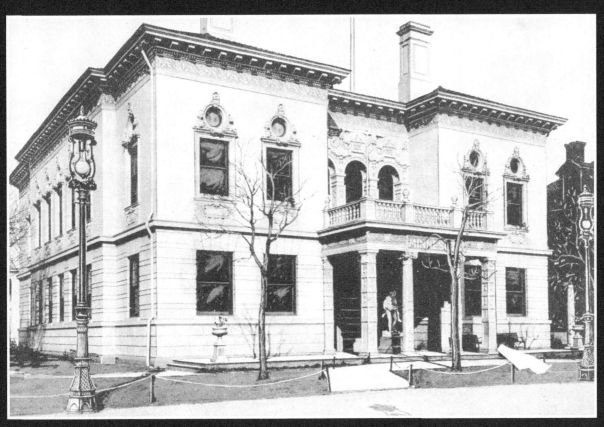

Minnesota Building.

Missouri Building.

Montana Building

Nebraska Building

Rhode Island Building

Virginia Building

Wisconsin Building.

Texas Building.

Michigan Building.

South Dakota Building.

Washington Building.

Avenue of State Buildings.

Ohio Building.

Florida Building.

Vermont Building.

California Building

The States Buildings.

The United States Government Building.

Viking ship in front of The U.S. Government Building.

United States Government Building

Livestock Pavilion.

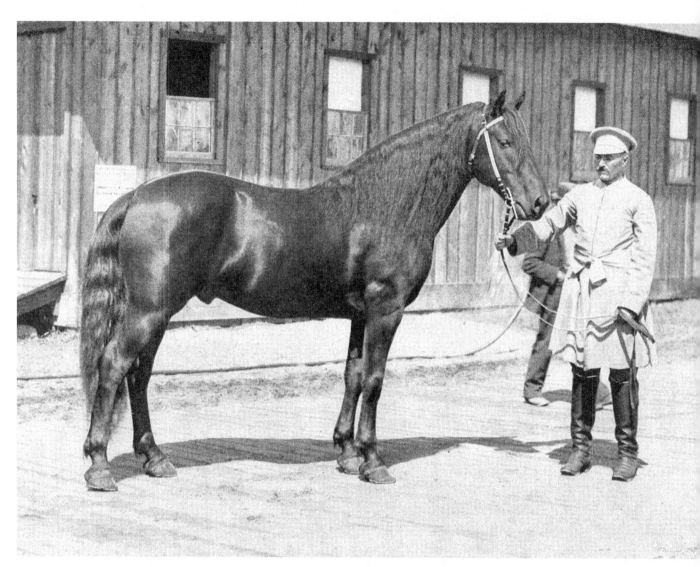

Horse being tended in the Livestock Arena.

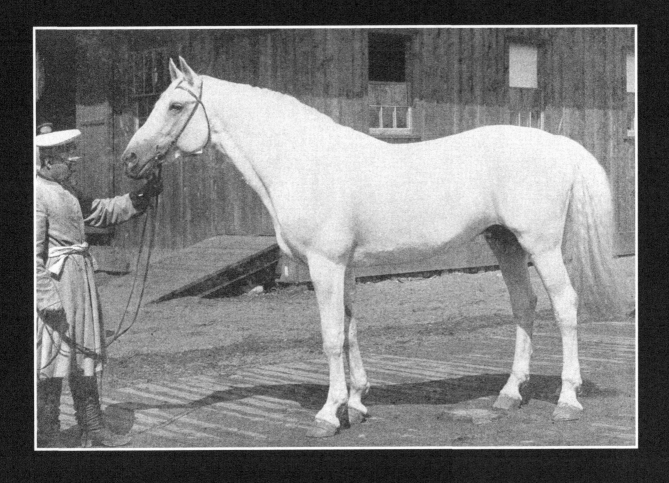

ABOUT THE AUTHOR

Mark Bussler is a writer, artist, and filmmaker specializing in video game, history, and science fiction related projects across a broad spectrum of media. Mark created **Classic Game Room** in 1999, and it remains the longest-running Internet video game review show in the world.

He writes retro game collecting and review guides based on the Classic Game Room museum archives. Mark is also the creator, writer and artist of several comic book series including *Ethel the Cyborg Ninja, Heyzoos the Coked-Up Chicken, Lord Karnage, Magnum Skywolf, Surf Panda, Retromegatrex* and *Seatropica*. He draws digitally using a combination of iPad Pro and Wacom tools in Adobe Photoshop.

Mark lives in deep space with his family, a broken computer and loyal dog. In 2004 he produced and directed the documentary film, **Expo: Magic of the White City** with Gene Wilder.

Follow Mark Bussler on Amazon for new book updates!

www.Amazon.com/author/MarkBussler

Subscribe to all my channels!

www.ClassicGameRoom.com
www.Amazon.com/v/ClassicGameRoom
www.Patreon.com/ClassicGameRoom
www.Instagram.com/ClassicGameRoom
www.Twitter.com/ClassicGameRoom

Mark's T-Shirts can be found on Amazon.com by searching
TURBO VOLCANO

Other Books from Classic Game Room Publishing

Ultra Massive Video Game Console
Guide Volume 1

Ultra Massive Video Game Console
Guide Volume 2

Ethel the Cyborg Ninja Book 1

The Story of the Ship

The White City of Color:
1893 World's Fair

Retromegatrex Volume 1: The Lost
Art of Mark Bussler 1995-2017

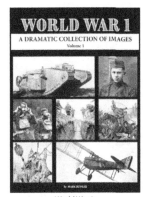

World War 1:
A Dramatic Collection of Images

New York 1908

Official Guide to the
World's Columbian Exposition

The World's Fair of 1893
Ultra Massive Photographic
Adventure Vol. 1

The World's Fair of 1893
Ultra Massive Photographic
Adventure Vol. 2

The World's Fair of 1893
Ultra Massive Photographic
Adventure Vol. 3

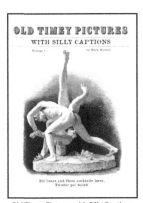

Old Timey Pictures with Silly Captions

Pac-Man Collector's Guide:
A Definitive Review

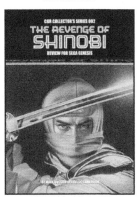

CGR Collector's Series 002:
The Revenge of Shinobi Review

The Great War Remastered WW1 Standard History Collection

Continued in Volume 2!

Made in the USA
Las Vegas, NV
28 April 2024

89239943R00184